Cambridge **Discovery Education**™

▶ **INTERACTIVE READERS**

Series editor: Bob Hastings

THE MAGIC OF MUSIC

A2

Genevieve Kocienda

CAMBRIDGE
UNIVERSITY PRESS

DISCOVERY
EDUCATION™

CAMBRIDGE UNIVERSITY PRESS
Cambridge, New York, Melbourne, Madrid, Cape Town,
Singapore, São Paulo, Delhi, Mexico City

Cambridge University Press
32 Avenue of the Americas, New York, NY 10013-2473, USA

www.cambridge.org
Information on this title: www.cambridge.org/9781107665583

First published 2014
Reprinted 2014

Printed in Hong Kong, China, by Golden Cup Printing Company Limited

A catalog record for this publication is available from the British Library.

Library of Congress Cataloging-in-Publication Data

Kocienda, G.
 The magic of music / Genevieve Kocienda.
     pages cm. -- (Cambridge discovery interactive readers)
  ISBN 978-1-107-66558-3 (pbk. : alk. paper)
 1. Music--Juvenile. 2. English language--Textbooks for foreign speakers. 3. Readers
(Elementary) I. Title.

ML83.K58 2013
781.1'7--dc23

                                   2013024141

ISBN 978-1-107-66558-3

Additional resources for this publication at www.cambridge.org

Layout services, art direction, book design, and photo research: Q2ABillSMITH GROUP
Editorial services: Hyphen S.A.
Audio production: CityVox, New York
Video production: Q2ABillSMITH GROUP

Contents

Before You Read:
Get Ready!

Music can make us feel happy or sad, excited or quiet. It can help us be healthy in our body, head, and heart. There is music everywhere in the world, and all people – and some animals – make music.

Words to Know

Look at the pictures. Then complete the sentences with the correct words.

audience

composer

conductor

perform

sound

❶ When you _____ , you sing, dance, or play music in front of other people.

❷ The _____ writes music.

❸ The _____ helps many musicians play well together.

❹ If something makes a(n) _____ , you can hear it.

❺ The people in the _____ listen to musicians play music.

Read the paragraphs. Then complete the sentences with the correct highlighted words.

What do you need to make a song? First, you need musical instruments to make sounds. Then the sounds must be in a rhythm that can be fast or slow. You also need musicians and singers to perform it. Finally, it's good to have an audience to listen to the song and to enjoy it. The sounds and rhythms in different songs can make people feel different emotions, such as happiness or sadness.

Songs are important for animals, too. Male animals need to find a female mate. Some male animals use songs to attract a mate. Many animals use songs for other kinds of communication, for example, to tell other animals about danger.

1 The ways you feel are your _____ .

2 Talking to someone is an example of _____ .

3 A song with a fast _____ can make you feel happy.

4 Most animals need a _____ to make babies.

? PREDICT

What was the first musical instrument?

CHAPTER 1

Why Music?

WHAT IS THE ORIGIN, OR BEGINNING, OF MUSIC?
WHAT IS MUSIC – AND WHY DO WE LISTEN TO IT?

Think about what people do when they hold a baby. They usually sing a song or make musical sounds, don't they? Well, scientists[1] know that mothers in every country, who speak different languages, do the same thing when they hold their babies. They all use a high **voice**, and they all make the same sounds again and again. These sounds have a rhythm and are like the **melody** of a song.

Scientists think that mothers made the same sounds to their babies in ancient[2] times. These sounds were, and are, very important for mother-child communication. Were these sounds the first songs? Perhaps.

[1] **scientist:** a person who studies any kind of science
[2] **ancient:** thousands of years ago

What is the origin of the first musical instrument?

More than two million years ago, ancient humans[3] used sharp rocks to cut like a knife. But when two rocks hit together, they can make a nice sound. So maybe rocks were the first percussion[4] instruments.

Over time, ancient humans made other instruments, too. In 1995 in Slovenia, a scientist found a flute made from the leg bone of a bear. The famous "Divje Babe" flute is about 50,000 years old. In a cave in southwestern Germany, scientists have found flutes that are at least 35,000 years old.

Some scientists think that people used music, and moving to music, as a way to feel the same emotions and work together.

....

[3] **human:** a man, woman, or child
[4] **percussion:** make sound by
  hitting, like a drum

Flutes

CHAPTER 2

Musical Places

THERE ARE MANY PLACES IN THE WORLD WHERE MUSIC IS AN IMPORTANT PART OF THE CULTURE.[5]

Some people like to go to big concerts. But many people prefer to hear music close up and to see the singers and musicians. If they are closer to the music, they can feel the emotions better.

This is what happens in Japan's "live houses." A live house is a very small room, sometimes under a restaurant or shop, for musicians to play in. Musicians who are not famous but are talented[6] play in these small places. They don't make very much money for playing music, but they get to play for an **audience**. People go there just to hear the music – not to eat, drink, or talk to their friends. There are about 300 live houses in Tokyo and about 1,000 live houses in all of Japan.

[5] **culture:** the ideas, language, art, and celebrations of one group of people
[6] **talented:** can do something very well

Buskers, musicians who play music on the street for money, have been around for a long time. The first buskers may have been traveling musicians who brought news and messages from one place to another. They also entertained[7] by singing songs for something to eat or a place to sleep.

Today in Mexico City, hundreds of mariachi bands play on the streets in a kind of daily **audition**. They hope that people will like their music and pay them to play at parties.

Every year there are many busker festivals[8] and competitions around the world. Ferrara, Italy, has one of the largest festivals, where thousands of buskers perform. In New York City, USA, only a few hundred buskers can play in the subway. So, every year, thousands of musicians audition in the *Music Under New York* competition to become one of the lucky few.

[7] **entertain:** perform for other people's enjoyment
[8] **festival:** special performances with many performers

EVALUATE
Why do people become buskers?

Music is a big part of Indian "Bollywood" movies. Audiences go to hear the music as much as to watch the movie.

Sometimes Bollywood songs tell us about the thoughts and emotions of one or more of the characters[9] in the movie. Sometimes they show us something that will happen later in the movie. The music and the words to the songs help explain the story and why the characters do what they do.

Most of the actors in a Bollywood movie don't sing. They lip sync[10] while they dance. Later, talented playback singers sing the songs. The playback singers are as famous as the actors. Many people go to see a movie just to hear their favorite playback singer. People can buy the soundtrack – the songs from the movie – before the movie comes out.

[9] **character:** a person in a story, like Harry Potter in J.K. Rowling's books
[10] **lip sync:** move your mouth with the music like you're singing, but you're not really singing

New Orleans, a city in the USA, is a very musical place. It is the home of jazz music.

Louis Armstrong playing the trumpet

In 1900, people from many different countries lived in New Orleans. And they all brought different kinds of music from their countries. The African-American musicians in New Orleans took these different kinds of music and mixed them with African rhythms to make a new music – jazz.

An important part of jazz is improvisation.[11] For part of the song, all the musicians play their instruments together. But then at different points in the song, one musician improvises while the others keep playing the rhythm and melody of the song.

One of the greatest jazz musicians was Louis Armstrong. This trumpet player from New Orleans is often called the father of jazz improvisation.

[11] **improvisation:** playing music that isn't written down. It is composed and played at the same time.
[12] **professor:** a teacher at a university

Video Quest

Jazz in New Orleans

Watch this video about Louis Armstrong. Did the professors[12] find Armstrong's first trumpet?

CHAPTER 3

Animal Rhythms

PEOPLE LOVE MUSIC, BUT WHAT ABOUT ANIMALS? CAN ANIMALS MAKE MUSIC? DO THEY ENJOY IT?

Nature makes beautiful sounds. And some music can sound like nature, like the wind or rain or an animal. The famous 18th-century composer Mozart, for example, wrote part of one of his songs for the piano to sound like the song of his pet bird.

So, humans sometimes write music to sound like animals or nature. But some scientists say that animals **compose** songs, too. For example, bird songs can sometimes have the same rhythm and pitches[13] as human music. And birds don't only sing, some of them "play the drums." Woodpeckers use their long, thin beaks against a tree to make quick, loud, rhythmic noises. The Ruffed Grouse moves its strong wings to make its drumming song.

[13]**pitch:** how high or low a musical sound is

A woodpecker uses its beak to make music.

The Ruffed Grouse uses its wings to make music.

Why do birds sing? They sing to find family members, give information about food, and tell other birds when there is danger. And, like humans, they sing to find love. In fact, birds that can compose the best songs are the first to attract mates.

Different birds have different songs for different jobs. For most of us, it is difficult to tell one kind of bird song from another. But some people know which bird is singing and what it is singing about. One famous birder, Ted Parker, could identify[14] more than 4,000 different kinds of bird songs!

[14]**identify:** correctly say what something is

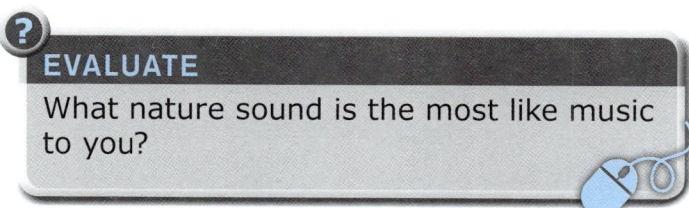

?

EVALUATE

What nature sound is the most like music to you?

A humpback whale

Birds are not the only animals that sing. For example, humpback whales spend a lot of time singing to each other. Their songs can last for many hours and can travel many kilometers under the water. Their songs are like human songs in some ways. They have rhythm, melody, and a structure – a beginning, a middle, and an end.

Male humpback whales sing alone or in a group. Some scientists think that they sing to attract a mate, but other scientists disagree. One thing all scientists know is that male humpback whales in the same ocean sing the same song – even if they live very, very far away from each other. And, when whales from one part of the world change their song, whales from other parts of the world change their song in the same way. Scientists don't know why or how this happens.

Big whales may sing to find love, but so do tiny[15] mice.

Tiny mice can sing.

You probably know what a mouse's squeak sounds like. But did you know that mice can sing? Like a bird's song, a mouse's song has many different sounds and rhythms. Mice sing to communicate with their brothers and sisters. However, they have a different song – a love song – when they want to attract a mate.

Many animals sing, but only the orangutans of Borneo make a musical instrument. They take the leaves off a tree, put them over their mouth, and

Orangutans can make an instrument from leaves.

make a kissing sound. The orangutans use this special sound to tell other orangutans that there is danger. This instrument makes the orangutan's call louder so other orangutans can hear it better.

....

[15]**tiny:** very small

Video Quest

The Alligator's Bellow

Watch this video to learn about the loud sounds that alligators make. Why do they make these sounds?

CHAPTER 4

The Joy of Music

MUSIC CAN MAKE US FEEL MANY DIFFERENT EMOTIONS.

Do you listen to music when you are sad? Does your favorite song make you feel good? Maybe you listen to music when you feel sick. Does the music help you feel better?

Around 400 BCE, Hippocrates, the Greek "Father of Medicine," played music for his **patients**. In ancient times, people in China, Egypt, India, and Rome also used music to help sick people get better. In World War I and World War II, doctors played music for soldiers who had emotional problems because of fighting in the war.

And today, many doctors still use music to help people. For example, some doctors play music for patients in the hospital after surgery.[16] It helps their bodies heal.[17] If patients listen to Mozart, maybe they will need less medicine.

[16] **surgery:** when a doctor cuts into a body to make someone better
[17] **heal:** become healthy

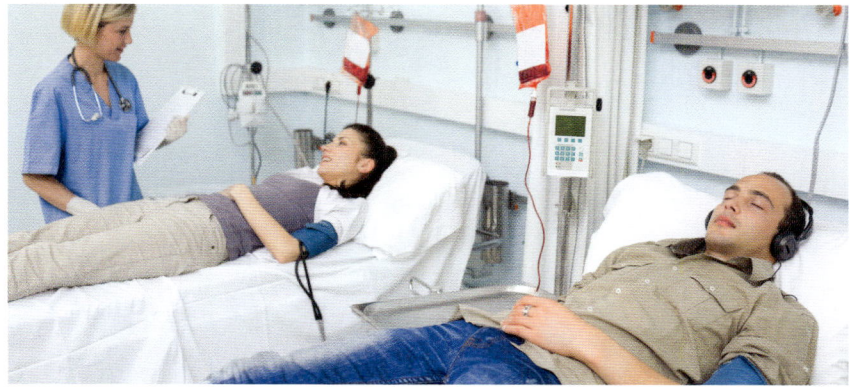

What happens when we listen to music? And why does it make us feel so many different emotions? As humans, we need food, water, and love from other people to live. But do we *need* music?

In one scientific study, different people listened to different kinds of music while scientists looked at what happened to the listener's body. When a person liked a song, the heartbeat[18] was faster and the body became warmer. Also, the brain made more dopamine. Dopamine is a chemical that gives us a good feeling.

With this study, scientists learned that music can make us feel good.

[18]**heartbeat:** the regular movement of the heart
[19]**soul:** the part of a person that is thought to control the feelings

Video Quest

Mariachi

Watch this video about the mariachi bands of Mexico. Why is mariachi music called "the soul[19] of Mexico"?

What happens when our lives are difficult? Can music still be a part of life?

Clive Wearing is a British conductor and pianist. In 1985, he became very sick and lost his memory. Now he can't remember anything of his past life. To make things worse, he can only remember a few seconds of time. After about 10 seconds, he forgets what happened before. For example, if his wife leaves the room and comes back 20 seconds later, he doesn't know who she is.

This makes his life very difficult. He needs a lot of help to live. However, there is one thing that Wearing can remember. He can still play the piano and **conduct** a choir.[20] He just can't remember how or when he learned to do these things!

---

[20] **choir:** a group of singers

Clive Wearing

Vibrations

Deaf people can enjoy music, too. Ludwig van Beethoven, for example, began to lose his hearing around age 30 and was completely deaf by his late 40s. But he continued writing and playing music. He went on to become one of the world's greatest composers.

When Beethoven's Ninth Symphony was played for the first time, he was so deaf that he could not hear the audience's loud **applause**. Someone turned Beethoven around so that he could see the audience. When he saw the people applauding, he cried.

How can deaf people enjoy music if they can't hear it? They can feel the vibrations in their brains when music is played. These vibrations happen in the same part of the brain other people use for hearing. In this way, a deaf person can enjoy music, too.

Derek Paravicini

CHAPTER 5

What Do You Think?

FOR SOME PEOPLE, MUSIC HAS ALWAYS BEEN A VERY IMPORTANT PART OF THEIR LIVES.

Derek Paravicini is a famous musical prodigy.[21] He was born about three months early and has some very serious learning problems. Also, he's blind – he can't see. But, when he was two years old, he started to play the piano. He had his first big concert when he was only nine. He can play any song after he hears it just one time. In fact, people call him the "Human iPod"!

Yo-Yo Ma, another child prodigy, started playing the cello when he was four. When he was seven years old, he performed for US President John F. Kennedy. Today, he is one of the most famous musicians in the world and has made more than 75 albums.[22]

[21] **prodigy:** a person who is very good at something at a very young age
[22] **albums:** a group of songs or pieces of music on CD, etc.

Why do you think music is important to Paravicini and Yo-Yo Ma? Do you think they hear and feel music differently from you? Why do both men play music? Why did they choose to play their instruments? Why not another instrument?

How about you? Do you play an instrument or sing? Why did you choose that instrument? If you don't play an instrument, do you want to learn to play an instrument or sing? Which instrument sounds the most beautiful to you?

Or would you like to be a music composer or conductor? Why or why not?

What kind of music do you listen to? Who is your favorite singer or musician? Do you like to listen to music at home, or do you like to go to concerts?

Yo-Yo Ma plays the cello.

After You Read

True or False?

Read the sentences and choose Ⓐ (True) or Ⓑ (False).

1 The first songs might be the sound that babies make.

Ⓐ True

Ⓑ False

2 Scientists have found a flute that is about 50,000 years old.

Ⓐ True

Ⓑ False

3 People can eat dinner in one of Japan's "live houses."

Ⓐ True

Ⓑ False

4 A busker plays on the street for money.

Ⓐ True

Ⓑ False

5 Many people go to New Orleans to hear jazz music.

Ⓐ True

Ⓑ False

Video
6 Alligators bellow when they are hungry.

Ⓐ True

Ⓑ False

Video
7 Mariachi music is played at many kinds of events.

Ⓐ True

Ⓑ False

8 Male humpback whales only sing alone.

Ⓐ True

Ⓑ False

Match

Match the vocabulary with the correct descriptions.

1 composer _____
2 sound _____
3 rhythm _____
4 perform _____
5 emotion _____
6 communication _____
7 mate _____
8 conductor _____

a it can be fast or slow
b an animal sometimes makes a noise to attract one of these
c someone who writes music
d something that you can hear
e something that you feel
f someone who helps musicians play well together
g telling another person what you think or how you feel
h sing in front of other people

Music Choices

Imagine that you have a friend who is sick or a friend who is sad. Think of some songs that can help. Why did you choose these songs?

Songs for a sick friend:

_____
_____
_____
_____

Why I chose these songs:

_____
_____
_____
_____

Songs for a sad friend:

_____
_____
_____

Why I chose these songs:

_____
_____
_____

Answer Key

Words to Know, page 4

1 perform **2** composer **3** conductor **4** sound
5 audience

Words to Know, page 5

1 emotions **2** communication **3** rhythm **4** mate

Predict, page 5
Answers will vary.

Evaluate, page 9
It is a way for them to make money and maybe become famous.

Video Quest, page 11
They are not sure.

Evaluate, page 13
Answers will vary.

Video Quest, page 15
They bellow to find a mate.

Video Quest, page 17
Mariachi music is the sound of many different emotions – of love, of joy, and also of sadness. It is in the heart of the Mexican people.

True or False?, page 22

1 B **2** A **3** B **4** A **5** A **6** B **7** A **8** B

Match, page 23

1 C **2** D **3** A **4** H **5** E **6** G **7** B **8** F

Music Choices, page 23
Answers will vary.